THE WEAPONS ENCYCLOPÆDIA
TANK AIRCRAFT AFV SHIP ARTILLERY VEHICLES SECRET WEAPON

TWE-019 ENG

USA TANK M3 LEE/GRANT

THE WEAPONS ENCYCLOPAEDIA

EDITORIAL STAFF
Luca Stefano Cristini, Paolo Crippa.

ACADEMIC EDITORIAL STAFF
Enrico Acerbi, Massimiliano Afiero, Aldo Antonicelli, Ruggero Calò, Luigi Carretta, Flavio Chistè, Anna Cristini, Carlo Cucut, Salvo Fagone, Enrico Finazzer, Arturo Giusti, Björn Huber, Andrea Lombardi, Aymeric Lopez, Marco Lucchetti, Gabriele Malavoglia, Luigi Manes, Giovanni Maressi, Francesco Mattesini, Péter Mujzer, Federico Peirani, Alberto Peruffo, Maurizio Raggi, Andrea Alberto Tallillo, Antonio Tallillo, Massimo Zorza.

PUBLISHED BY
Luca Cristini Editore (Soldiershop), via Orio, 33/D - 24050 Zanica (BG) ITALY.

DISTRIBUTION BY
Soldiershop - www.soldiershop.com, Amazon, Ingram Spark, Berliner Zinnfigurem (D), LaFeltrinelli, Mondadori, Libera Editorial (Spain), Google book (eBook), Kobo, (eBoook), Apple Book (eBook).

PUBLISHING'S NOTES
None of unpublished images or text of our book may be reproduced in any format without the expressed written permission of Luca Cristini Editore (already Soldiershop.com) when not indicate as marked with license creative commons 3.0 or 4.0. Luca Cristini Editore has made every reasonable effort to locate, contact and acknowledge rights holders and to correctly apply terms and conditions to Content. Every effort has been made to trace the copyright of all the photographs. If there are unintentional omissions, please contact the publisher in writing at: info@soldiershop.com, who will correct all subsequent editions.

LICENSES COMMONS
This book may utilize part of material marked with license creative commons 3.0 or 4.0 (CC BY 4.0), (CC BY-ND 4.0), (CC BY-SA 4.0) or (CC0 1.0). We give appropriate attribution credit and indicate if change were made in the acknowledgments field. Our WTW books series utilize only fonts licensed under the SIL Open Font License or other free use license.

CONTRIBUTORS OF THIS VOLUME & ACKNOWLEDGEMENTS
Ringraziamo i principali collaboratori di questo numero: I profili dei carri sono tutti dell'autore. Le colorazioni delle foto sono di Anna Cristini. Ringraziamenti particolari a istituzioni nazionali e/o private quali: Stato Maggiore dell'esercito, Archivio di Stato, Bundesarchiv, Nara, Library of Congress ecc. A P.Crippa, A.Lopez, L.Manes, C.Cucut, archivi Tallillo. Model Victoria (www.modelvictoria.it), per avere messo a disposizione immagini o altro dei loro archivi. Wikipedia CC1 by Bukoved.

For a complete list of Soldiershop titles, or for every information please contact us on our website: www.soldiershop.com or www.cristinieditore.com. E-mail: info@soldiershop.com. Keep up to date on Facebook & Twitter: https://www.facebook.com/soldiershop.publishing

Title: **U.S.A. MEDIUM TANK M3 LEE/GRANT** Code.: **TWE-019 EN**
Series by Luca Stefano Cristini
ISBN code: 9791255890713. First edition January 2024.
THE WEAPONS ENCYCLOPAEDIA (SOLDIERSHOP) is a trademark of Luca Cristini Editore

THE WEAPONS ENCYCLOPÆDIA
TANK AIRCRAFT AFV SHIP ARTILLERY VEHICLES SECRET WEAPON

U.S.A. MEDIUM TANK M3 LEE/GRANT

LUCA STEFANO CRISTINI

BOOK SERIES FOR MODELERS & COLLECTORS

CONTENTS

Introduction 5
- Development and design 6
- Technical features 9

Operational use 23
- North African front 23
- Russian front 32
- The war in the Pacific 33
- Burma campaign 37
- Australian campaign 38

Camouflage and distinctive signs 41
- Last period 42

Versions of the vehicle 47

Conclusion 52

Data sheet 52

Bibliography 58

▼ The characteristic silhouette of the M3 Lee, lacking, moreover, the machine gun dome.

INTRODUCTION

Officially designated as Medium Tank, M3 was a U.S. medium tank actively employed during World War II. Its turret was made in two variants, one in accordance with U.S. specifications and the other modified to meet British requirements, in this case including the placement of the radio next to the commander. In the context of the British Commonwealth, the tank acquired two distinct designations: those with U.S.-modeled turrets were called "Lee," in tribute to Confederate General Robert E. Lee, while those with British-model turrets were identified as "Grant," in honor of Union General Ulysses S. Grant, the two major and famous American generals of the Civil War.

Widely used during the course of the conflict, it initially gave good proof on the North African front where it proved superior to Panzer III and Italian M14/41 tanks, while it could fight on a par with early versions of Panzer IVs. But by 1943 its limitations became increasingly obvious and it was soon replaced by the M4 Sherman. Despite its remarkable performance in the early part of the war, the M3 Lee/Grant never achieved the same fame as the Sherman. This fact can be attributed to its origins and the role it played during the conflict; born as a surrogate for the failed M2 Medium Tank (1938), which never crossed American borders, the M3 was conceived, designed, and produced with a certain urgency. In 1939, at the beginning of the conflict in Europe, the United States was not yet ready for action. Tank design was still evolving in a period of peace and post-conflict context, thus maintaining a tactical thinking inherited from World War I that would soon be superseded.

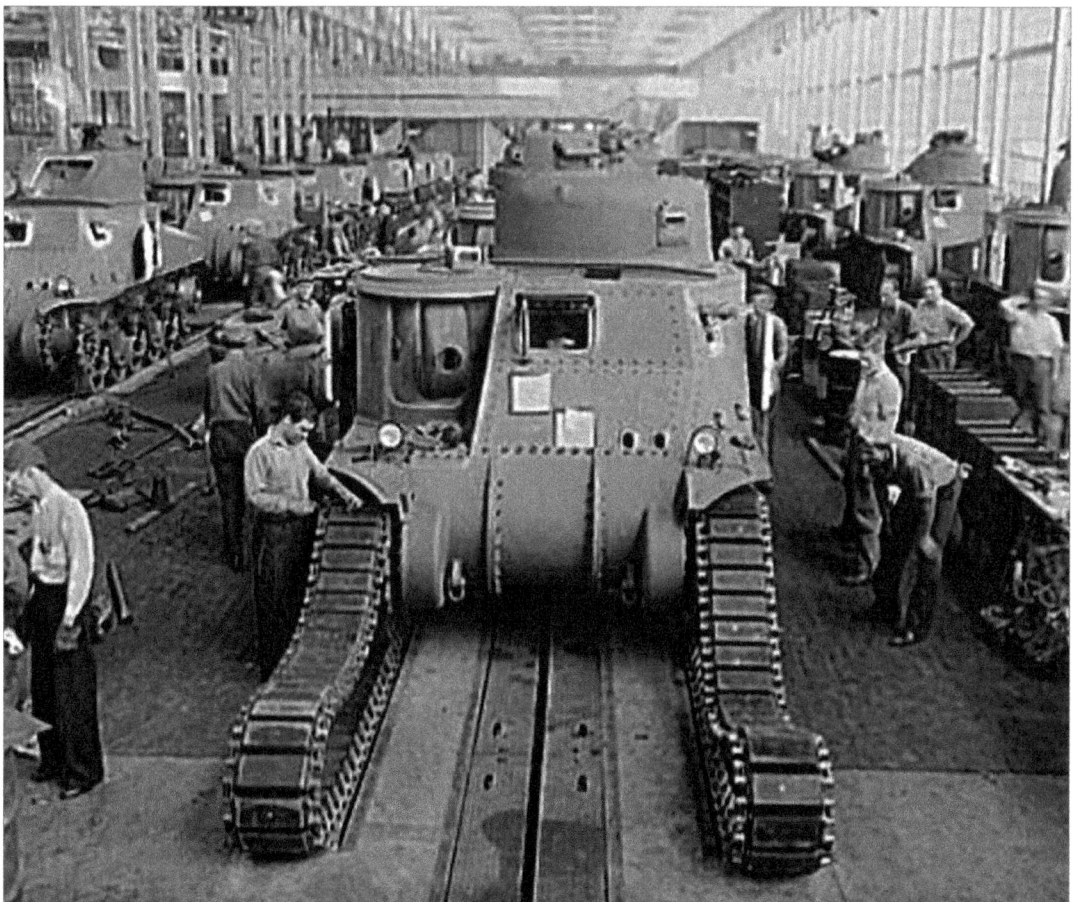

▲ M3 tank assembly chain at Detroit Tank Arsenal in 1942.

DEVELOPMENT AND DESIGN

The unexpected blitzkrieg triggered in France during World War II was a surprise that, in reaction, triggered a complete overhaul of U.S., and Allied ingeneral, tank design. Soon after the conclusion of the Air Battle of Britain, the theater of war expanded to North Africa. British industry, with a nation largely tested by near international isolation, could not produce enough tanks to defend both the motherland and the scattered territories of the empire, especially such crucial points as the Mediterranean and the Suez Canal. With the passage of the Rent and Loan Act on March 11, 1941, President Roosevelt proclaimed the United States as "the arsenal of democracy." In this context, the M3 Lee quickly became the emblem of this strange de facto alliance, its most tangible symbol.

The design process for the M3 began in July 1940, and the first examples became operational in late 1941. The U.S. Army needed a robust medium tank armed with a 75 mm cannon, and, considering also the immediate and vital demand of the nearly 4,000 medium tanks from the United Kingdom, production of the Lee began as early as late 1940. The resulting design of the armored vehicle was a compromise aimed at producing a tank as soon as possible, intended to serve only until it was replaced by the later M4 Sherman tank, which was already in production.

As mentioned in the introduction, it was basically an enlarged M2, but equipped with better armor, a much taller and wider hull, all to enable the tank to come armed with a 75 mm (2.95-inch) gun placed in a casemate located on the right side. The 75 mm was to deal with both static land targets and act as a counter-tank, thanks to its armor-piercing projectiles and good speed. High explosive projectiles were also tested and later used. However, the standard 37-mm (1.46-inch) cannon was still preferred in the anti-tank role, so a solution was found to add this second weapon in a small turret atop the superstructure.

▲ The armor plate on the M3 was too heavy for welding and had to be riveted in place. Wikipedia CC1

M3 Mk.1 Lee medium tank first production, U.S. 1941

▲ Insertion of the R-975 engine into its compartment on the assembly line. Author's coloring.

The first M3 prototype was completed in March 1941. Construction began immediately at the Detroit Arsenal of Chrysler, American Locomotive and Baldwin Locomotive as early as a month later, in April 1941. By the summer of that year the tank was in full production, leading to the tank being built in excess of 6,000 units from April 1941 to December 1942. The M3s that came off the production lines, while reminiscent of the "parent" M2, had squarer and taller silhouettes, and were equipped with three pairs of suspensions on each side of the tank.

Both the U.S. tanks and those produced for the British featured thicker armor than originally planned. The British design required one less crew member than the U.S. version because of, as mentioned earlier, the presence of the radio in the turret. The U.S., in fact, opted to eliminate the figure of the radio operator, assigning the task directly to the commander. After the first field battles, which resulted in substantial losses in Africa and Greece, the British understood that, to meet their armored needs, they would have to adopt both the American Lee type and their own Grant type.

The M3 was a reliable tank with considerable firepower, excellent armor, and high mobility, but it had serious drawbacks in its overall design and form, including its excessive silhouette, an awkward and impractical main gun arrangement that prevented the tank from assuming a defensive position in many situations, and finally its archaic rivet construction.

According to Hans von Luck, a German army officer who authored the postwar memoirs reported in his famous book-diary "Panzer Commander" (published by Soldiershop Publishing, ed.), the M3 was considered by the German General Staff to be superior even to the Panzer IV in May 1942, as well as being able to operate outside the range of the German 5-cm anti-tank guns. However, in mid-1943, with the introduction of the new and upgraded Panzer III and IV, the tank was soon withdrawn from combat in most theaters of operation and replaced by the more capable M4 Sherman tank as soon as it became available in larger quantities.

Despite its replacement occurring almost everywhere, the British continued to employ M3s in combat against the Japanese in Southeast Asia until 1945. Nearly a thousand M3s were also supplied to the Soviet Army under the Rent and Loan program between 1941 and 1943.

■ TECHNICAL FEATURES

In the engineers' initial ideas, the design included an upper dome to accommodate a 7.62 mm caliber machine gun, giving this tank hybrid an almost sci-fi and caricatured appearance, and similar to a comic book character, with guns protruding from turrets, from the sides a bit everywhere, more like a navy battleship. This design, after all, was in line with the practice of U.S. tanks of the time, the secondary armament comprising three to eight Model 1919 7.62 mm caliber machine guns. To facilitate and speed up production, vital to Britain's livelihood, the tracks, most of the suspension system, wheels and return rollers had all been borrowed from the earlier model already referred to as, again, its parent, namely the M2 tank. The main difference lay mainly in the new three-bogie train and redesigned suspension.

▲ Structure of the 75 mm cannon as it was mounted on the M3 Lee/Grant tank in the Royal Australian Corps Tank Museum, Puckapunyal, Victoria, Australia. Wikipedia CC1 courtesy by Bukoved.

M3 Grant Mk.I 1st British 1st Armored Division Medium Tank, North Africa, 1942

The M3 was born very wide and spacious, being able to accommodate a transmission unit that ran through the passenger compartment. The transmission components were mammoth. The synchronized gearbox offered 5 forward gears, one reverse, while steering typically came via differential braking. The vertical volute suspension incorporated a self-contained return roller, now no longer attached to the hull, simplifying any maintenance and repair work. The turret, operated by an electrohydraulic system powered by the main engine, provided full and very fast rotation; in less than 15 seconds it operated 180° on itself and included a stabilizer for the main gun.

The Grant's turret armor was welded, but the Lee's turret and the rest of both tanks were riveted. The thickness of the armor reached the good measure of 56 mm at the thickest part. The armament in this wild card tank was clearly a temporary fix in both choice and assembly.

The 75 mm cannon was one of the most powerful weapons in the world at the time, capable of being able to use high-explosive and armor-piercing projectiles. However, the weakness of the M3's cannon was its limited maneuverability.

The main cannon was operated by two men: a loader and a gunner who operated the fork-handled weapon; a view was provided through an M1 telescope mounted on the roof of the casemate that housed the cannon. The main cannon had a maximum range of 2,700 m. The tank was also equipped with a secondary cannon arranged in the 37-mm turret, also fitted with an M2 telescope and a maximum range of 1400 m, operated with gear-driven steering wheels for translation and elevation. Standard equipment inside the vehicle included 46 rounds for the 75-mm cannon, 178 for the 37-mm cannon, and 9,200 for the machine guns.

▲ Men at work in Chrysler Arsenal, near Detroit, assemble tracks to a giant M3 Lee.

M3 Mk.1 Lee Tank No. 3 Medium Tank, F Company,
2nd Tank Battalion USA, 13th Armoured Regiment USA - 1st Armoured Division USA, USA 1942

▲▼ After final assembly, the plant's control personnel carry out a thorough inspection.
Below: detail of the rolling train of the M3 Lee tank.

M3 Mk.1 Lee medium tank version with cast Turtle Back hull and M2 gun with counterweight. Armoured Force School at Fort Knox, Kentucky, USA 1942

The 37 mm cannon was already an obsolete piece at the time of its use on the M3, but the wagon required an upper turret with a 360-degree traverse and a reasonably powerful cannon in an anti-tank function. The result was that the Grant, which started out as a transitional tank, had one gun designed for the present and another for the future.

There were also further shortcomings: the main one, as already mentioned, was that the 75 mm cannon was positioned in a low part of the wagon, moreover angled to one side, which meant that the vehicle could not fire its main gun from the position favoured by the tank crew, i.e. from a central turret, or as the Anglo-Saxons say: 'hull down'. Another weakness of the 75 used was its relatively poor longevity, a far cry from artillery standards that required such a piece to be able to fire at least 4,000 rounds before going to the workshop for repairs. Unfortunately, this was not the case with the cannon mounted on the M3! Decreasing the rate of fire, i.e. the speed, increased the life of the piece but made it less effective at piercing the armour of a German tank.

On the positive side, however, the Grant had some advantages besides its two guns: if necessary, the petrol engine could be replaced by safer Chrysler diesel engines. The maintenance and repair of this armoured pachyderm was rather simple.

The original configuration of the vehicle envisaged machine guns mounted on the upper turret, lower co-axials, on the commander's cupola, a rear external anti-aircraft mount for a single and even four machine guns, mounted at the four corners of the structure, which, however, rarely came into use in practice.

The wagon was also very versatile and responsive; this power was made possible by a nine-cylinder Wright Continental nine-cylinder petrol-powered radial aero engine, which provided enough power to propel the 30-tonne wagon up to 26 miles per hour on the road or 16 miles off-road. The weak point was that the 100 octane petrol used on the wagon was highly flammable, and the wagon could explode if it was hit. The ove-

▲ Detail of the M3 turret. Model exhibited at the Yad la-Shiryon Museum, Israel. Wikipedia by Bukoved.

rall design was among the tallest in its class, reaching up to 3m. This oversizing was its main disadvantage on the battlefield. There was no shortage of irony about this giant: the Germans nicknamed it 'splendid target', while the Americans called it 'the iron cathedral'.

▲ The ancestor of the Lee/Grant was essentially the M2A3 wagon pictured here in April 1939 in Washington. Above, small photo: another view of the assembly line in the production facilities.

▲ The M3 tank crew trains on the new vehicle during manoeuvres held at Camp Polk in February 1943. Above: photo of the tank next to an officer in full uniform.

USA TANK M3 LEE/GRANT

M3 Mk.1 medium tank Grant Australian 1st Armoured Division, Puckapunyal, June 1942

USA TANK M3 LEE/GRANT

▲ In the United States, the tank underwent intensive testing and personnel training. Pictured: an M3 Lee tank in the Californian desert at the Training Centre, Indio, Calif, on 6 October 1942. Nara US archives.
Author's colouring.

M3 Mk.1 medium tank Grant, British Eight Army, Gazala, Libya, June 1942

▲ M3 Lee tanks of the US Army's 1st Armoured Division in Louisiana during extended exercises in the southern states in September 1941. Note the old British helmets still in place.

▼ The same exercises always in the USA. This photo almost looks like something out of a Holywood movie....

▲ 'Factory' photograph of one of the first M3 tanks just out of the oven.

▲ Beautiful picture of an M3 Lee tank engaged in test runs on semi-desert terrain.

OPERATIONAL USE

A Due to the British armed forces' desperate need for armoured forces, the M3 represented one of the most complicated hybrids of the entire war. Created through the US lease and loan agreement, the tank was a *de facto* dual nationality, dual designations, dual equipment and an endless variety of uses. Used extensively during the Desert War, particularly in North Africa, it gradually lost importance with the arrival of new, more reliable wagons.

■ NORTH AFRICAN FRONT

The M3 played an important role in increasing the firepower of British forces during the North African desert campaign. The first Grants were sent directly to Egypt and at the time lacked certain equipment (such as radios), which were later integrated locally. As part of the 'Mechanisation Experimental Establishment (Middle East)', other modifications were tested, approved and made to the tanks as they were being supplied to the front line. These included the installation of sand shields (later deliveries from the USA were already assembled this way), dust covers for the gun shrouds and the removal of excess machine guns from the hull. The ammunition arrangement was changed to 80 75mm rounds (a significant increase of 30 more rounds) and 80 37mm rounds with additional protection for the ammunition containers.

The Grants arrived in North Africa in late January 1942 and the British crews immediately began training. As the 75 mm cannon used was derived from a French model from the First World War, the British could rely on a fair supply of ammunition left over from that time, although these had suffered deficien-

▲ A British Grant on the left and a Lee M3 on the right on the battlefield of El Alamein (in the Egyptian Western Desert) in 1942. This image allows one to observe the different British turret from the original one.

M3 Mk.1 Lee 'Battleship II' medium tank of the British 8th Armoured Brigade, 10th Armoured Division, North Africa, October 1942

cies and loss of efficiency due to age. The armour-piercing projectile for the 75mm cannon was a massive ball and could penetrate about 50mm of armour if fired from less than 1,000m, improving performance over the 2lb British tank guns, but this was still not enough. Fortunately for the British, large quantities of German 75 mm shells were captured during some engagements and these were immediately adapted to the American cartridge. This conversion ensured improved performance, which was later followed up by a new American design of the armour-piercing projectile (the M61). Although the Grant was expected to be an emergency solution (this imprinting characterised the American tank from the outset) at least until the Crusader Mark III tank with a 57 mm 6-pounder cannon became available, once the new British tank was ready, it unfortunately presented a number of problems, which prevented the Grant from being retired for the time being! The Grant therefore remained the main wagon in use and Crusader wagons such as the Crusader Mk I and II only replaced the M3 light tank in British units.

The first battle use of the M3 tank came in 1942, during the North African Campaign. British Lee and Grant tanks were used against Rommel's forces in the Battle of Gazala on 27 May of that year. In preparation for the battle, the Eighth Army received as many as 167 M3 tanks. The 8th King's Regiment Royal Irish Hussars and the 3rd and 5th Battalions of the Royal Tank Regiment immediately went into action with their Grant tanks. Retreating in the face of a major German attack, the 8th Hussars Regiment was left with only three of its Grants, while the 3rd RTR suffered the loss of 16 Grants.

Their appearance, however, came as a surprise to the Germans, who were unprepared for the M3's 75 mm cannon. They soon discovered to their cost that the M3 tank could engage them beyond the effective range of their 5 cm Pak 38 anti-tank gun and the 5 cm KwK 39 of the Panzer III, their main medium tank. The M3 tank was also clearly superior to the Italian Fiat M13/40 and M14/41 tanks employed by the Italian troops, whose 47 mm guns were only effective at close range, while only the few 75/18 self-propelled guns were capable of destroying the Grant tank using HEAT projectiles.

▲ Ammunition supply to an M3 Grant in North Africa, 18 June 1942.

▲ The ingenious camouflage of the M3 tank disguised as a truck with a cloth structure.

▲ The original M3 Grant used by British Field Marshal Montgomery, now on display at the Imperial War Museum in London. It was present at the Battle of El Alamein.

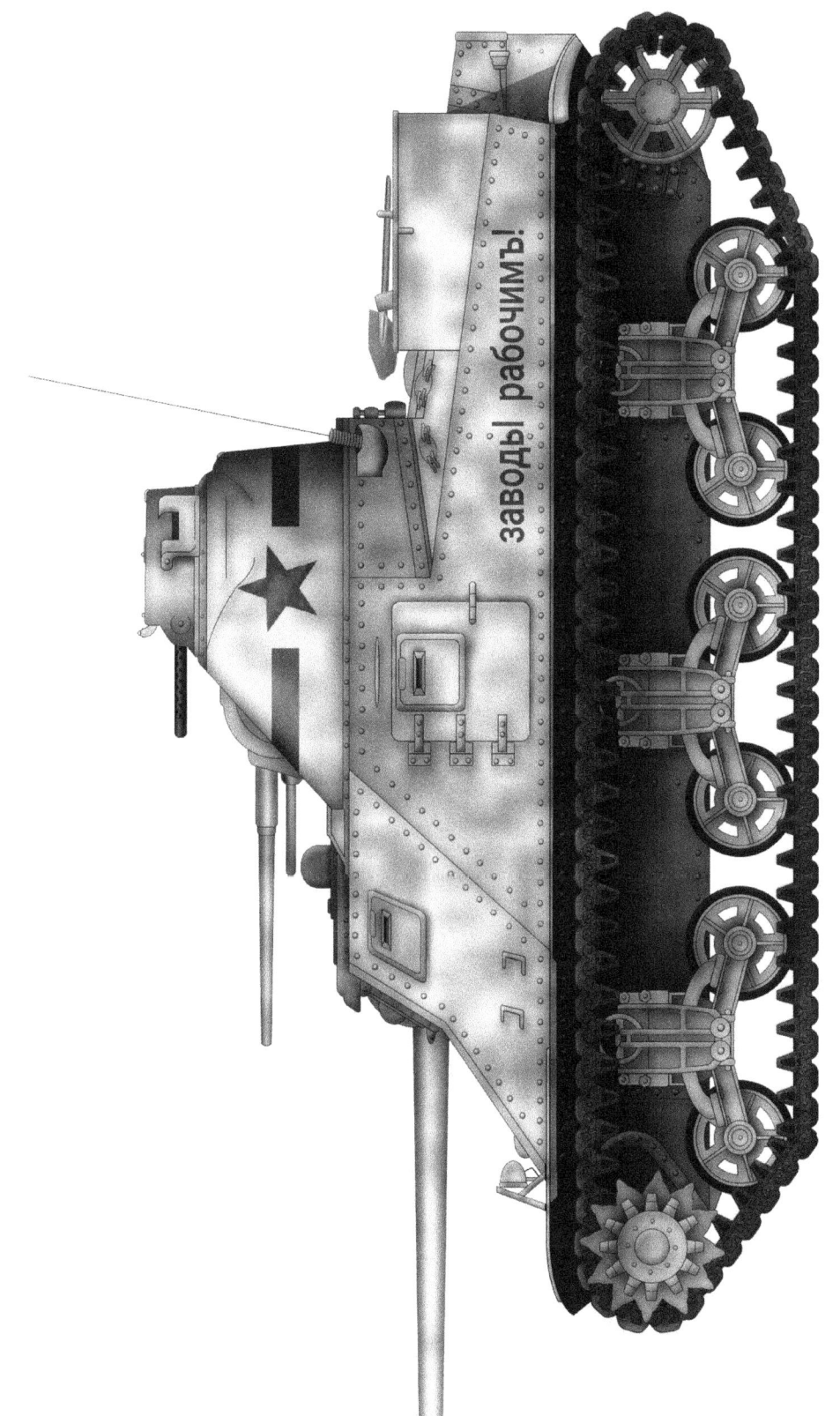

M3S Mk.1 Lee medium tank of the 241st Armoured Brigade
Stalingrad, Russia, October 1942

M3 tank Mk.1 Grant British Eight Army, El Alamein, November 1942

In addition to the longer range of the M3, the vehicle was equipped with high-explosive projectiles to eliminate infantry and other soft targets, which the earlier British tanks did not possess; with the introduction of the M3, Rommel noted: *"Until May 1942, our tanks were generally superior in quality to the corresponding British types. Now this was no longer true, at least not to the same extent."*

Despite the M3's advantages and its striking appearance during the Battle of Gazala, it failed to secure victory for the British. In particular, the effective 88 mm anti-aircraft gun, used in its secondary role as an anti-tank gun, proved lethal for all British tanks, bar none, especially if they attacked without artillery support. However, Britain's Director of Armoured Vehicles stated before the arrival of the M4 Sherman that: *"The Grants and Lees have proved the mainstay of fighting forces in the Middle East; their great reliability, powerful armament and solid armour have endeared them to the troops."*

At the Second Battle of El Alamein in late 1942, there were over 600 M3s, of both types, in British service. More of these were in the UK for training.

▲ Still the same M3 tank on page 26, with only half the camouflage structure, which allows one to see the lightness of the structure to conceal the armoured vehicle.

The Grants and Lees served with British units in North Africa until the end of the campaign. Following Operation Torch (the invasion of North Africa), the United States also fought in North Africa using the M3 Lee. The US 1st Armoured Division had received the new M4 Sherman, but had surrendered an entire regiment of the new vehicles to the British Army so that it could use them in the Second Battle of El Alamein (October-November 1942). Consequently, one regiment of the division was still using the M3 Lee tank when it arrived in North Africa.

The M3 was generally appreciated throughout the North African campaign for its mechanical reliability, good armour protection and superb firepower. In all three aspects, the M3 tank was able to engage German tanks and towed anti-tank guns. However, the high silhouette and the low, side-mounted 75 mm cannon on the hull were tactical disadvantages as they prevented optimal combat in many cases, especially from a concealed firing position. Furthermore, the use of riveted armour on the superstructure in the early models led to spalling, where the impact of enemy bullets caused the rivets to detach, which in turn became deadly projectiles inside the tank. Later models were built with fully welded armour to eliminate this problem. These lessons were all applied to the design and production of the new M4.

The M3 was replaced in frontline roles by the M4 Sherman as soon as the latter became available. However, several specialised vehicles based on the M3 were later deployed in Europe, such as the M31 armoured recovery vehicle and the Canal Defence Light. In early 1943, British Eighth Army M3 tanks, now replaced by the Sherman, were sent to fight the war in the Pacific against the Japanese to replace some Matildas in the Australian Army.

▲ American crew of an M3 near Souk el Arba, Tunisia, 23 November 1942.

M3 Mk.1 Lee Operation Torch medium tank - US Army - November 1942

RUSSIAN FRONT

From 1941, 1,386 M3 medium tanks were sent from the United States to the Soviet Union, with as many as 417 of them lost in transit (when they sank with the ships carrying them, hit by submarine, naval and German aircraft attacks en route). These were provided through the American Rent and Loan programme between 1942 and 1943.

Like British Commonwealth units, Soviet Red Army personnel tended to refer to the M3 as the 'Grant' tank, although all M3 tanks shipped to Russia were actually variants of the 'Lee'. The official Soviet designation was М3 средний (М3с), or 'M3 Medium', to distinguish the Lee from the US-built light tank M3 Stuart, which was acquired by the USSR, again through the Rent and Loan programme, and officially known as М3 лёгкий (М3л), or 'M3 Light'.

Due to the vehicle's petrol engine, its high propensity to catch fire and its vulnerability against most German armoured vehicles encountered by Soviet troops from 1942 onwards, the tank was very unpopular in the Red Army from its introduction on the Eastern Front.

With almost 1,500 Russian T-34 tanks being built every month, Soviet use of the medium M3 tank soon lost importance shortly after mid-1943. Soviet troops nevertheless deployed their Lee/Grant tanks on secondary and less active fronts, such as in the Arctic region during the Red Army's Petsamo-Kirkenes offensive against German forces in Norway in October 1944, where the obsolete US tanks faced mainly old captured French tanks used by the Germans, such as the SOMUA S35, which to a limited extent was somewhat comparable to the Lee/Grant it fought against.

▲ An M3 Lee company in column of the Soviet 6th Guards Army as it advances towards the front line during the Battle of Kursk, July 1943.

THE WAR IN THE PACIFIC

In the Pacific War, armoured forces played a relatively marginal role for both the Allies and the Japanese, when compared to naval, air and infantry units. In the Pacific Ocean and Southwest Pacific Theatre, the US Army deployed none of its dedicated armoured divisions and only a third of its 70 autonomous tank battalions.

A limited number of M3 Lee were used in the Central Pacific Theatre in 1943, partly because the US Marine Corps did not use the M3 Lee; they switched directly from M3 Stuarts to M4 Shermans in mid-1944. Some M3 Grants instead played an offensive role with the British-serving Indian Army operating in the south-east Asian theatre.

The Australian Army also used Grants during World War II, mainly for home defence and training purposes.

The only wartime use of the M3 Lee by the US Army against Japanese forces occurred during the Gilbert and Marshall Islands campaign in 1943.

Following the most notorious landing at Tarawa, the US 27th Infantry Division carried out an amphibious assault on Makin Island with the armoured support of a platoon of M3A5 Lee equipped with deep fords kits belonging to the US Army's 193rd Tank Battalion.

▲ An M3 Lee tank complete with its original dome, its crew proudly displaying ammunition destined for the enemy. Photo Nara archive USA.

▲ View of the M3 Lee/Grant Mk I tank from above.

▲ View of the M3 Lee/Grant Mk I tank from front.

▲ View of the M3 Lee/Grant Mk I tank from behind.

BURMA CAMPAIGN

After British Commonwealth forces in Europe and the Mediterranean began receiving M4 Shermans, some 900 M3 Lee/Grant ordered by Britain were sent to the Indian Army. Some of them went into action against Japanese troops and their tanks in the Burma Campaign during World War II.

Still used by the British Fourteenth Army until the fall of Rangoon, they ended up doing 'admirable' work in their originally intended role of supporting infantry in Burma between 1944 and 1945.

In the Burma Campaign, the M3 medium tank's main task was infantry support. It distinguished itself and played a key role during the Battle of Imphal, during which the Imperial Japanese Army's 14th Tank Regiment (equipped mainly with its own Type 95 Ha-Go light tanks, along with a handful of captured British M3 Stuart light tanks) clashed for the first time with British M3 medium tanks, which outgunned and outclassed their light tanks. The British M3 tanks did well in crossing the steep hills around Imphal where they defeated the attacking Japanese forces. Officially declared obsolete in April 1944, the Lee/Grant nevertheless remained in action until the end of the war in September 1945.

▲ A British M3 Lee tank supported by Indian infantry in Mandalay, Burma (Myanmar), during the Burma campaign in March 1945.

AUSTRALIAN CAMPAIGN

At the start of the war, Australian Army doctrine regarded armoured units as minor offensive components within infantry divisions. It did not have an ad hoc armoured corps and most of its limited capabilities in armoured warfare had already been employed in the North African Campaign (within three divisional cavalry battalions). Towards the beginning of 1941, the effectiveness of large-scale German panzer attacks was finally recognised and a dedicated armoured division was formed to counter it. The Australian Armoured Corps initially included the cadres of three armoured divisions, all of which were equipped at least in part with M3 Grants made available from surplus British orders. The 1st Australian Armoured Division was formed with the intention of supplementing the three Australian infantry divisions present in North Africa. However, following the outbreak of hostilities with Japan, the division was retained in Australia. Between April and May 1942, meanwhile, the regiments of the 1st Armoured Division were being re-equipped with M3 Grants and were training in a series of large exercises in the area around Narrabri. The cadres of the other two divisions, the 2nd and 3rd Armoured Divisions, were officially formed in 1942, as Militia (reserve/internal defence) units.

These divisions were also partly equipped with M3 Grants. In January 1943, the main body of the 1st Armoured Division was deployed for home defence duties between Perth and Geraldton, where it was part of III Corps. Towards the middle of the war, the Australian Army judged the Grant unsuitable for overseas war tasks and the units that had used the M3 wagon were re-equipped with the Matilda II before being deployed in the New Guinea and Borneo Campaigns. Due to personnel shortages, all three divisions were officially disbanded in 1943 and downsized to brigade and battalion level units.

▲ View of the Australian Yaramba tank derived from the M3, at the Royal Australian Armoured Corps Tank Museum.

Medium tank M3 Mk.1 'Monthy' Grant 8th Army Tactical HQ, Tripoli, January 1943

M3A2 Lee medium tank of the 13th US Armoured Reg. 1st AD in Tunisia, January 1943

CAMOUFLAGE AND DISTINCTIVE SIGNS

During World War II, the United States Army Corps of Engineers was responsible for the camouflage of military vehicles and developed a series of manuals (FM) and other instructions for this purpose. The purpose of these manuals was to instruct the leaders of the Engineer Battalions to use these colours appropriately and to adopt the camouflage patterns indicated. The two most significant manuals were the following: FM 5-20 and FM 5-21, published in October 1942. During the war, the US Army Engineer Corps specified several colours, which we quote here along with their Federal Standard Equivalent:

- N. 9 Olive Drab
- N. 22 Olive Drab
- N. 8 Earth Red
- N. 6 Earth Yellow
- N. 5 Earth Brown
- N. 1 Light Green
- N. 31 Olive Drab
- N. 11 Forest Green
- N. 10 Black
- N. 12 Desert Sand
- Ocean Gray
- Olive Drab 50.

The background colour par excellence, which came into being in the 1930s, was Olive Drab (OD) No. 22. The same one that later became No. 9 from 1942. Olive Drab in the broadest sense had been the basic colour of the USA since 1917. The shade of Olive Drab used by the USAAF was darker than that of the Army and was designated as Olive Drab No. 31. This shade was not unified with the Army's because it had a specific anti-infrared characteristic.

Olive Drab colour shades underwent several changes during the course of the war, but not the colour specifications, which remained unchanged since the 1920s. In the years leading up to the Second World War, the colours appeared in an opaque tone, whereas by the end of the war it had evolved into a more satin-like tone, almost glossy in some cases.

The colour also changed in brightness; at the beginning of the war the shade was lighter than at the end of the war. Variations were also due to the different paint manufacturers, who had different shades of Olive Drab, ranging from yellow to brown. As already mentioned, the Olive Drab used towards the end of the war had a sheen characteristic and the shade was more brown, making for a very different hue from that seen at the outbreak of the Second World War.

The Marine Corps used colours that were more complementary to those used by the Army, such as colour No. 12 Desert Sand to camouflage their vehicles, as well as all the OD colour variants, Earth Yellow and Earth Red. The Marine Corps, like the Army, used Forest Green as the base colour for its M3 and M2A2 tanks, but never used the OD colour for the same vehicles. Also among the marines, some LVTPs and landing craft were painted in a grey colour called Ocean Grey.

The Army had a battalion that specialised in painting vehicles, while the Marine Corps relied on vehicle crews to apply the paint and any camouflage. This practice soon spread throughout the Corps, and the Marines took pride in it, as it allowed them a certain 'artistic' freedom in creating their camouflage.

During the Solomon Islands invasion, some very colourful camouflage models appeared.

WW2 USA TANK COLORS & CAMOUFLAGE

| Insignia White | Ocean Grey | White | Aged White | Ivory | US Sand | US Light Green |
| US Field Drab | US Olive Drab | US Forrest Green | US Earth Red | US Earth Brown | Black | UK Tommy Green |

In the army, the 1st Armoured Division was the first armoured unit deployed in Africa. Its vehicles were painted in Olive Drab, with large yellow stripes and stars. So flashy that the Germans called these tanks 'ideal targets'. In fact, during the first battles against the German forces it was soon realised that these colours were not a good choice in the desert environment. Consequently, American troops began using local sand and paint to camouflage their vehicles in the North African environment.

■ LAST PERIOD

It was only after the invasion of Sicily, otherwise known as Operation Husky, that the formal colours established by the Corps of Engineers were also used to camouflage vehicles in Africa. It was then that the complementary colours Earth Yellow No. 6 and Earth Red No. 8 began to be used.

Vehicles and armoured units operating in forests and hot climates had to be painted in Olive drab 50 and Black; both dark colours applied in a broad stripe pattern. Later, light green No. 1 was also added as a complementary colour. White was obviously used for camouflage in cold and arctic climates.

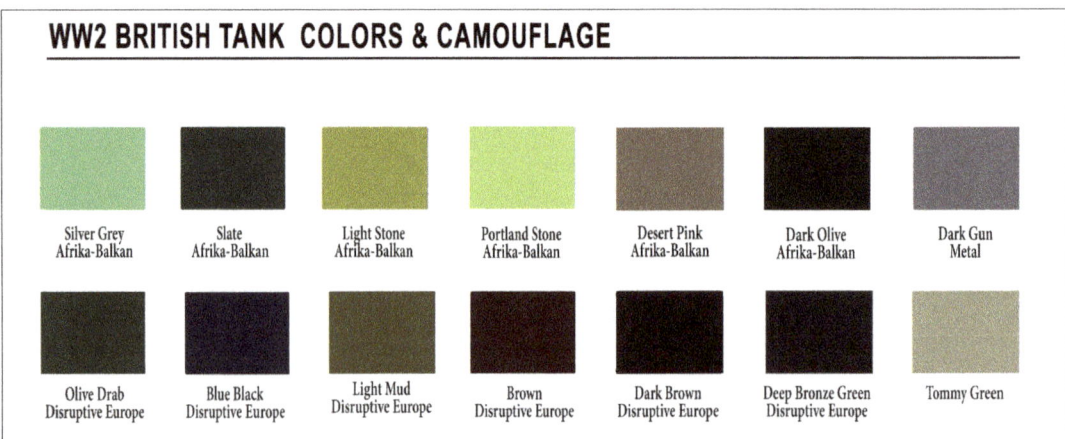

M3A2 Lee Medium Tank F company 12th Battalion 1st US Armoured Division, Tunisia, February 1943

▲ The M3 tank in its classic American Olive Drab livery.

▼ A Grant in full camouflage at El Alamein with the 8th Army, November 1942, displayed at Bovington.

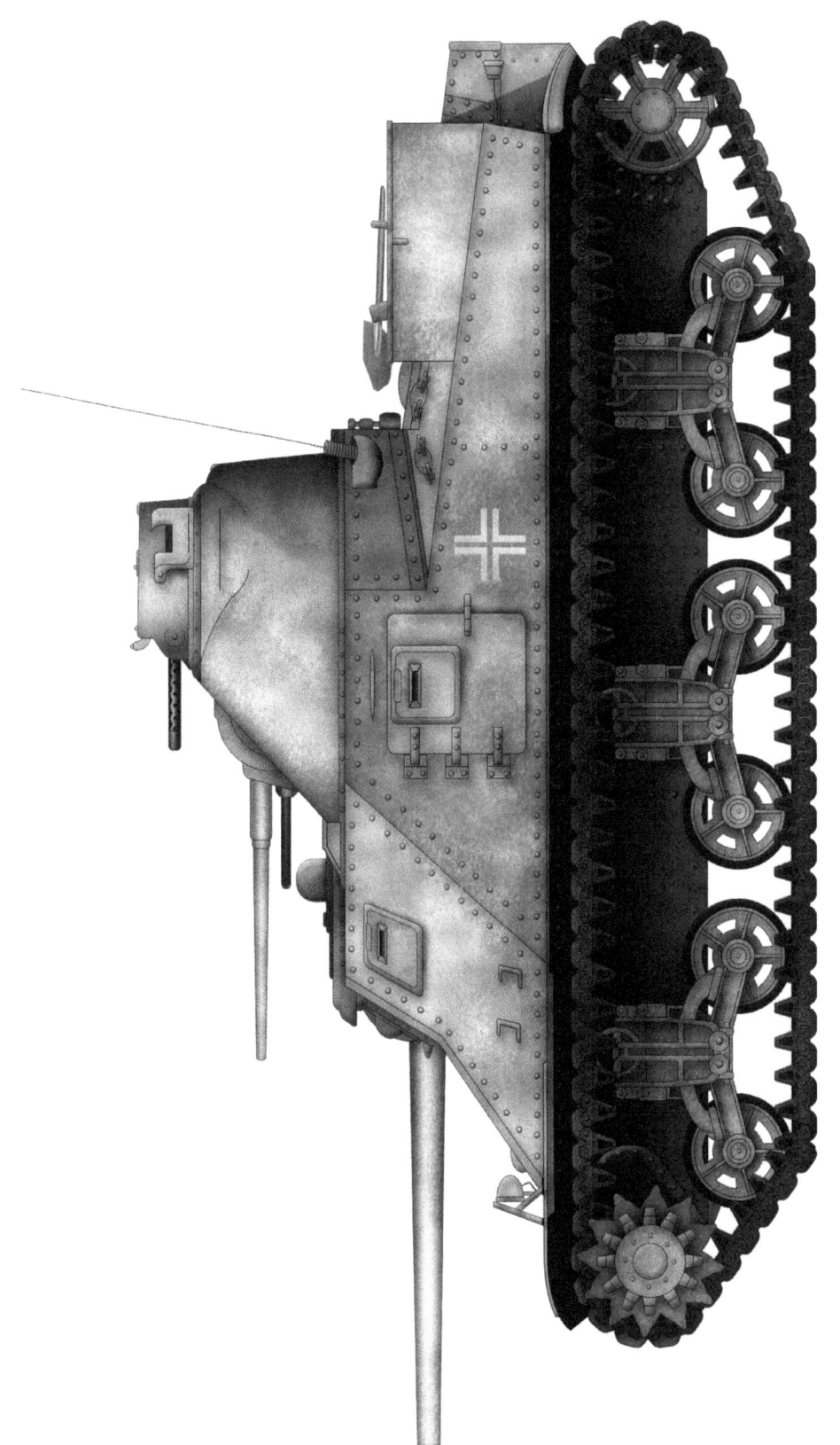

M3A2 Lee medium tank captured 'Beutepanzer' Russia, February 1943

Unidentified M3A2 Lee 'Beutepanzer' medium tank, Russia 1943-1944

VERSIONS OF THE VEHICLE

The M3 tank immediately provided an excellent basis for further development, and in this context enjoyed incredible success. Not only did it facilitate the faster design and production of the US Army's most strategically important tank, the M4 Sherman, of which it was certainly the parent, thanks to the many parts it shared with the M3. But the Grant/Lee did not only 'christen' the Sherman, but its chassis provided the basis for the creation of other vehicles. These vehicles included the Canadian Ram tank, the 105 mm (4.13 inch) M7 Howitzer Motor Carriage, also known as the M7 Priest, the 155 mm (6.1 inch) M12 Gun Motor Carriage, the Kangaroo armoured vehicle and the Sexton Mk.I gun-propelled tank.

Let us now look at the main variants used by the Americans, British and Australians:

UNITED STATES VARIANTS (in brackets the British name):

- **M3 (Lee I/Grant I)**: riveted sheet metal hull, high-profile turret, petrol engine 4,724 examples produced.

- **M3A1 (Lee II)**: cast hull (rounded edges). 300 examples produced.

- **M3A2 (Lee III)**: welded plate hull (sloping edges). Only 12 examples produced.

- **M3A3 (Lee IV/Lee V)**: welded hull, two GM 6-71 diesel engines coupled, side doors welded or removed. 322 examples produced.

- **M3A4 (Lee VI)**: elongated hull in riveted sheet metal, Chrysler A57 Multibank engine (21 litre displacement, five cylinders, 480 hp at 2,700 rpm), side doors removed 109 examples produced.

- **M3A5 (Grant II)**: riveted plate hull, two GM 6-71 diesel engines coupled. Despite being fitted with the original Lee turret, the British called it the Grant II. 591 examples produced.

▲ The recovery tank version was the most widely used. Cannons and machine guns were dummy simulacra.

- **M31 Tank Recovery Vehicle (Grant ARV I)**: recovery variant based on the M3 hull, with mock turret and 75 mm cannon, equipped with 27-tonne winch.
- **M31B1 Tank Recovery Vehicle**: based on M3A3 hull.
- **M31B2 Tank Recovery Vehicle**: based on M3A5 hull.
- **M33 Prime Mover**: M31 TRV converted to artillery tractors, with turret and crane removed. 109 examples converted between 1943 and 1944.
- **105 mm Howitzer Motor Carriage M7 (Priest)**: 105 mm M1/M2 howitzer on an M3 hull with an open superstructure. An unarmed version was used as an observation vehicle for artillery.
- **155 mm Gun Motor Carriage M12**: designed as T6, 155 mm M1917/1918M1 gun on M3 hull with open superstructure. 100 examples produced between 1942 and 1943.

An M30 Cargo Carrier version was also built on the same hull for transporting ammunition and servants.

BRITISH VARIANTS

- **Grant ARV**: cannons removed and replaced with armoured recovery vehicle equipment.
- **Grant Command**: command tank version equipped with map table and additional radio equipment, with guns removed or replaced by simulacra.
- **Grant Scorpion III**: 75 mm cannon removed, equipped with Scorpion III flail demining system. Made in a small number in early 1943 for use in North Africa.
- **Grant Scorpion IV**: Scorpion III with additional motor to increase the power of Scorpion flails.
- **Grant CDL**: photoelectric version, 37 mm turret replaced by the 'Canal Defence Light' system, equipped with a powerful searchlight and machine gun. 355 examples also produced by the Americans under the name **Shop Tractor T10**.

AUSTRALIAN VARIANTS

- **M3 BARV**: only one M3A5 was converted to BARV ("Beach Armoured Recovery Vehicle").
- **Yeramba Self Propelled Gun**: Australian self-propelled vehicle on M3A5 hull equipped with Ordnance QF 25 lb gun, similar conversion to the Canadian Sexton. 13 vehicles built in 1949.

▲ General Auchinleck and other officers observe the battle from the back of an M3 tank. Egyptian desert, 1942.

▲ Adapted British M3 tank with a searchlight on the turret, it was named Canal Defense Light.
▼ Australian model of M3 BARV a recovery tank for beach landings.

USA TANK M3 LEE/GRANT

▲ M3 Lee during a lunch break of her crew in North Africa, November 1942. Nara Archive

▼ ▶ Two pictures showing one of the most interesting versions made from M3 hulls, especially after its decommissioning as a tank. On the right an M12 operating in the Bayeux region June 1944. Below an M7 105 mm Howitzer Motor Carriage (Priest.)

Recovery tank M31 'GO GET IT' of an unidentified US unit, Sicily, July 1943

CONCLUSION

Summing up, the M3 was a vehicle that, with all its flaws but also thanks to its merits, was able to be effective on the battlefield from 1942 to 1943. This tank, however, was a plastic demonstration of the shortcomings of the US armoured units, which, having arrived late to the complex world of armoured vehicles, lacked tactical skills that did not allow it to quickly close the gap with the more modern German tanks. The Grant/Lee's armour and firepower were equivalent, if not superior, to most of the enemy tanks it faced, especially in the Pacific against the Japanese. Fortunately for it, long-range and high-speed weapons had not yet spread well on German tanks in the African theatre, the first real front on which the American tank clashed with the German enemy. Inevitably, the rapid development of tanks during the Second World War meant that the M3 was very quickly outclassed. In mid-1942, with the appearance of the deadly German Tiger I, and the upgraded armament of the Panzer IV now equipped with a 75 mm long gun, and from 1943 the arrival of other even more modern vehicles soon led to the disappearance of the M3 on the ground, but it was worthily replaced by its son: the Sherman M4!!

DATA SHEET	
	Grant/Lee M3
Length	5640 mm
Width	2720 mm
Height	3120 mm
Date of entry into service/exit	1941/1945
Weight in combat order	27,25 t
Crew	5/6 (commander, pilot, servants and gunner)
Engine	Continental R-975-EC2 petrol
Maximum speed	42 km/h on road 18 km/h off road
Autonomy	193 km on road, 90 off road
Maximum slope	34,5%
Armour thickness	From 15 to 50 mm
Armament	1 M3/M4 75 mm cannon (in casemate) 1 M5/M6 37 mm cannon 4 Browning M1919A4 cal .30 (7.62 mm) machine guns
Production	6.258 units

M3 Mk.1 Lee medium tank Canadian unit in Britain, October 1943

USA TANK M3 LEE/GRANT

MAIN USERS

Country	Quantity	Years	Notes
Australia	757 (end of 1942)	1942 – 1955.	Many versions used as well as local modifications
Brasil	104 (around 1944)	1942 – end of 1950	M3 and M31 TRV. Never used in combat. Some examples have been locally modified.
Canada	47 (May 1942)	1941 - 1942	In service with the 5th Armored Division. Never entered combat.
France	51 (March 1943)	In service in 1943	Tanks left to the French by the Americans at the end of the African campaign. Used for training.
USA	1.921	1941-1944	
Paraguay	nd	1950	Tanks obtained from Brazil.
UK	2.855 o 2.887		The second number includes Australian tanks.
URSS	1.386	1942 - 1945	Only 976 arrived, 410 ended up sunk on the journey.

M3 VERSION DESIGNATIONS

Names of the various versions and date of entry into production					
Anno	Motore	USA	UK (Lee)	UK (Grant)	URSS
June 1941	Gasoline	M3	General Lee I	General Grant I	M3S28
January 1942	Gasoline	M3A2	General Lee III	General Grant III	
January 1942	Diesel	M3A3	General Lee VII	General Grant VII	
January 1942	Diesel	M3A5	General Lee IX	General Grant IX	
February 1942	Gasoline	M3A1	General Lee II	General Grant II (not produced)	
not produced	Diesel	M3	General Lee IV	General Grant IV	
1942	Diesel	M3A1	General Lee V	General Grant V	
not produced	Diesel	M3A2	General Lee VI	General Grant VI	
June 1942	Gasoline	M3A4	General Lee VIII	General Grant VIII (not produced)	

Medium tank M3s Unknown Russian unit on the Leningrad front named 'Za Rodinu', 'for the fatherland', October 1943

M3A5 Lee medium tank in Burma, Squadron c 3rd Carabiniers regiment, 1944

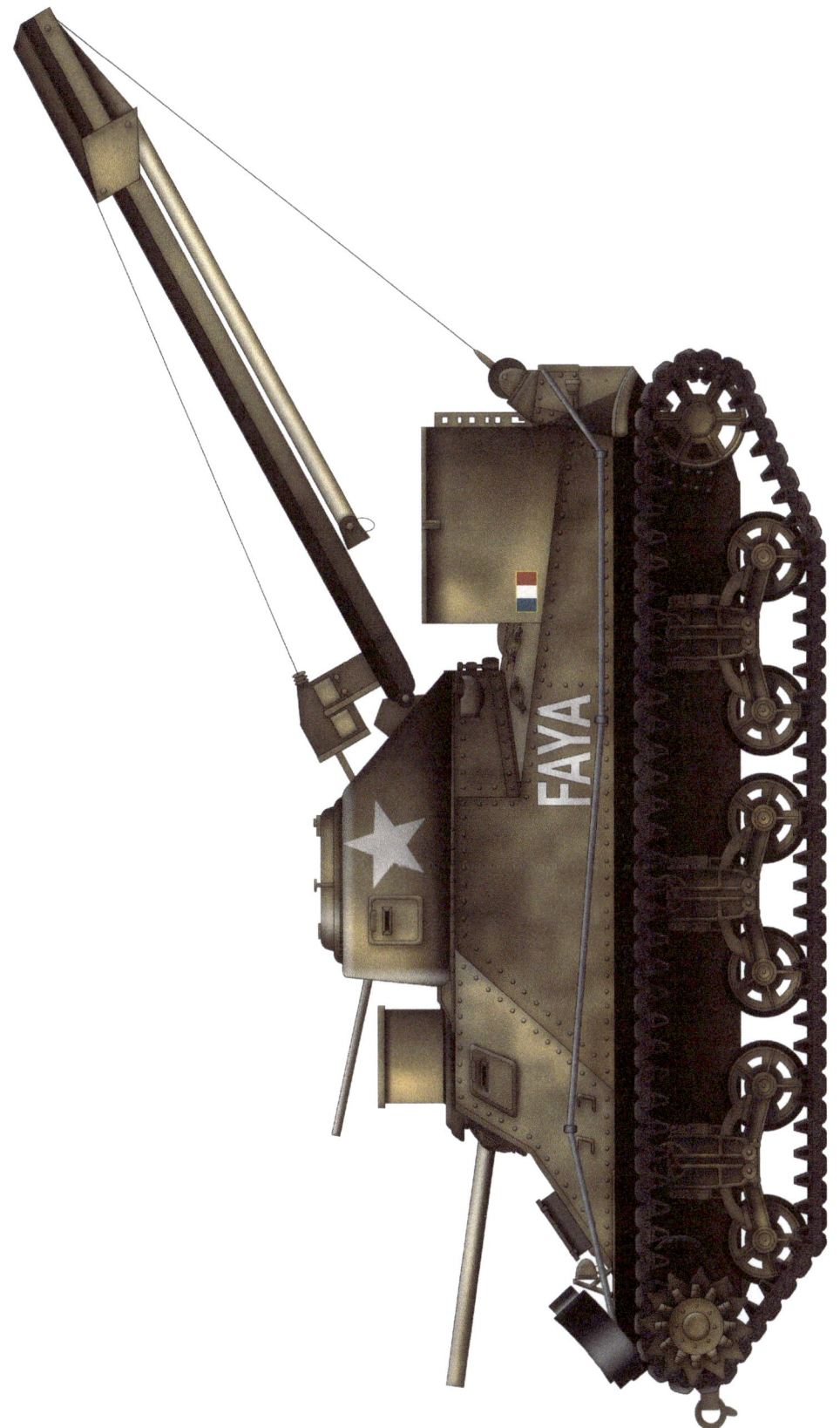

Recovery tank M31 'FAYA' French 2nd Armoured Division, Normandy, summer 1944

BIBLIOGRAPHY

- Bishop, Chris *The Encyclopedia of Weapons of World War II* (2002) Metro Books.
- Chamberlain, Peter; Ellis, Chris. *British and American Tanks of World War II*. New York: Arco.
- Chamberlain, Peter; Ellis, Chris. *M3 Medium (Lee/Grant). AFV Profile No. 11*. Windsor: Profile Publishing.
- Fletcher, David. *The Great Tank Scandal: British Armour in the Second World War - Part 1*. HMSO.
- Hunnicutt, R. P. Sherman, *A History of the American Medium Tank*. 1978; Taurus Enterprises.
- Porter, David *Allied Tanks of World War II (World's Great Weapons)* (2014) Amber Books
- USMC D-F Series Tables of Equipment (TOEs), 1942-1944
- Rottman, Gordon L. (2008). *M3 Medium Tank vs Panzer III: Kasserine Pass 1943. Duel No. 10*. Oxford: Osprey Publishing.
- Zaloga, Steven J. (2005). *M3 Lee/Grant Medium Tank 1941-45*. New Vanguard No. 113. Oxford: Osprey Publishing.
- Zaloga, Steven (2007). *Japanese Tanks 1939-45*. New Vanguard No. 137. Osprey Publishing.
- Zaloga, Steven (2008). *Armored Thunderbolt: The US Army Sherman in World War II*. Stackpole Books. ISBN 978-0-8117-0424-3..
- David Doyle *M3 Lee and Grant - the Design, Production and Service of the M3* DavidDoyleBooks
- David Doyle *M3 Medium Tank: The Lee and Grant Tanks in World War II (Legends of Warfare)* DavidDoyleBooks
- David Doyle *M3 Medium Tank Walk Around SS5712* Squadron- Signal .
- Zajaczkowski, Slawomi *Medium Tank M3 Lee / M3 Grant. M3A1, M3A2, M3A4, M3A5.* Kagero Polonia.
- Peter Chamberlain, Chris Ellis *AFV Weapons Profile 11 - M3 Medium Lee-Grant*
- Jim Mesko *M3 Lee/grant in action* Squadron - Signal
- Bryan Perrett *The LeeGrant Tanks in British Service* New vanguard Osprey
- Terry J. Gander - *Tanks in detail: Medium Tank M3 to M3A5 General Lee/Grant* 2003
- AA.VV - *M3 Lee/Grant* 108 Wydawnictwo Militaria Polonia.
- Zajaczkowski, Slawomir, *Medium Tank M3 Lee I (Top Drawings)*. Kagero Polonia
- Hans Halberstadt *Inside the Great Tanks* 1998 by The Crowood Press Ltd

ALREADY PUBLISHED TITLES

ALL BOOKS IN THE SERIES ARE PRINTED IN ITALIAN AND ENGLISH

VISIT OUR WEBSITE FOR MORE INFORMATION ON
THE WEAPONS ENCYCLOPAEDIA:
https://soldiershop.com/collane/libri/the-weapons-encyclopaedia/

TWE-019 EN

www.ingramcontent.com/pod-product-compliance
Lightning Source LLC
LaVergne TN
LVHW072122060526
838201LV00068B/4945